STONE GATHERING

A READER

for Bill

Contents

INTRODUCTION	10
ROSEMERRY WAHTOLA TROMMER Perhaps You Can Hear It?	15
OCTAVIO SOLIS *La Migra*	16
AARON BROWN Elegy	20
JOHN EDGAR WIDEMAN Witness	22
JULIE GARD Homage to Lydia Davis	23
JULIE GARD On Scarcity	24
DEBRA MARQUART Dylan's Lost Years	25
ROSS GAY What About That, Steve Jobs?	26
MARVIN BELL The Revolution Needs a Song	29

Contents

NANCY MILLER GOMEZ Growing Apples	30
KATHY FISH Collective Nouns for Humans in the Wild	31
WENDELL BERRY The Peace of Wild Things	32
JANE BROX Star Light, Star Bright	33
THOMAS C. STETZLER Meditation	36
THOMAS C. STETZLER Spectator	37
SIRI LIV MYHROM Peonies	38
DON SHEA Blindsided	40
ANDREW J. OLSON Razorburn	41
NICOLE BORG Out of Kansas	44

Contents

NAOMI SHIHAB NYE Kindness	46
LINDA LEGARDE GROVER The Refugees	48
EDWARD HIRSCH I Was Never Able To Pray	52
AFTERWORD	55
CONTRIBUTORS	57
PERMISSIONS	63
ABOUT THE EDITOR	67
ACKNOWLEDGEMENTS	69
ABOUT FRENCH PRESS EDITIONS	71

Introduction

My grandkids and I search our rocky shore for stones to paint and give away. *Kindness rocks* are a thing, you know. The children consider each stone, rub it somewhat clean, hold it up for all to see, briefly noting its smooth or creased face, its raised bumps or pocky divots. I say *briefly* because their imaginations have already run ahead—to the giving of each, to wondering whose hands might reach for color, for feel, for weight, for words they need to hear.

It strikes me that the work I do on this quarterly reader has much affinity with my grandchildren's project—hence, its title: *Stone Gathering*. And the example of *kindness rocks*, if pedestrian, may be just right for thinking about the power of literary short forms: how—like stones—these small writings can be pocketed, held, studied, meditated upon, shared, or kept as treasures. We are in sore need of such comforts and consolations at present.

While poetry has long been considered small enough and precious enough to tuck into your pocket (there is even a National Poem in Your Pocket Day), certainly the prose pieces collected here, these small fictions and essayettes, also belong in your literal or figurative pocket. For they have much in common with poems, especially with prose poems—even more, perhaps, than with the longer work in their own genres. This is because the art/the work of compressing language, of honing it to the fewest words that carry the most meaning, is a *poetic act*. And since we are all *by nature* poets, it's no wonder we respond to this compression, this honing, this beautiful, powerful, meaning-*full* language with all

STONE GATHERING

A READER

poems, small fictions, essayettes

DEBORAH JACOBS, SERIES EDITOR

Stone Gathering

A Reader

Volume One, Issue One   Summer 2019

Copyright © 2019 by Danielle Dufy Literary

All Rights Reserved

Layout and Design by Chip & Jean Borkenhagen,
River Place Press, Aitkin, MN

Printed at Bang Printing, Brainerd, MN

ISBN:978-1-7339423-0-0

First Edition

An imprint of
Danielle Dufy Literary

P.O. Box 334
Brainerd, MN 56401
www.danielledufy.com

equal strength. But even if that were possible, I don't suppose the night sky would conjure the tumult of feeling that rose up within me all those years ago. Abundant artificial light creates a different kind of night for the human spirit, one in which it's a simple thing to travel through the dark, and which can be full of leisure or as full of direction as day. As the dusk draws down, I merely have to flick a switch to continue with my work, and I only have to look out the window to feel the company of others doing the same.

The star-struck sky belongs to a spare world, unbounded and without distraction, where it's never a simple thing to take cover from the night, where every attempt to do so is small and self-conscious. Perhaps it's age and experience that make it so, or the rarity of it, but when I chance to see such a sky now—atop a mountain, along a deserted stretch of coast—it feels like a privilege as I fall through the years toward ancient time.

Meditation

by Thomas C. Stetzler

I wander this stream bed
gathering stones,
agate, mostly,
Apache tears,
rock mantras
to turn in the hand,
some cracked to reveal
deep patterns
that gleam in the canyon
when rain bursts
from the swollen sky
and the river lives.

Spectator

by Thomas C. Stetzler

Nolan wasted years
in a protective fetal posture
waiting for the darkness
to lose interest in him.

He was drawn along by time,
gleaned the consolation
of sunrises, meadows
of columbine.

At the end he was worn smooth
like a small stone
in the bed of a quiet stream.

Peonies

by Siri Liv Myhrom

Early June, and the peonies are here. They rest, very prim, in a Depression glass vase on the buffet, the glass a perfect tangy green that holds early summer light. The blushed petal scent is so thick with sweetness that I walk through it as I go by. They are something from another time.

I stop a moment with each pass, marveling at how a thing can be substantial and fragile at the same time, how layered they are, unfurling like the papery stacked sheets of a wasp's nest. And the ants that dutifully sip the sugary nectar that appears in droplets on the bud scales, unknowingly helping to gently pry open that immense, densely-packed bloom from the clenched fist. And the huge blossoms, so heavy that they droop on their too-thin stems, weighed down by so much beauty in their brief offering.

In all this witnessing, I miss my mom so much and wish she was here to see it all, too. These are from her yard. They didn't bloom last summer—the spring was dark and cool, and they were planted in a too-shady spot. So my dad transplanted them to the south side of the house, for my mom, even though she wasn't there to see them, just because she loved peonies and he loves her. They thrived this summer after her death, in their new sun-soaked bed, and I went over to water them and snip a few blooms for the house.

The missing is a space with edges. It snags in my throat as I pass through that dense aroma like a curtain. I probably believed at one time that grief was this rarified event, something separate and terrible that you go through to get back to your real, normal life. But I don't think I see it that way anymore.

It's all just living, and grief visits and is one way that we learn the same lessons over and over and over: that sorrow is not meant to be separated neatly out from the rest of life, but rather that we are made to braid together beauty and mess and missing and glory through each of our days; that it is okay to stop and be curious, even when the wound pools up in the midst of our wonder; that we're here to hold so much beauty that we can barely stand, so that all we can do is bow down and press our faces to the ground and pray, *Thank you, thank you. Show me how to be useful and loving and lovely. Thank you.*

Blindsided

by Don Shea

It started as a low, sweet jumble of sound, whiny and country, from the far end of the subway car. Then you could make out a small, pale man of middle years and thinning hair shuffling forward through the passengers with a dog by his side and a sack on his back containing a radio or tape player from which this strangely sweet country sound—a voice, a guitar and fiddle—was spilling out and he was singing along with it, singing along with his own voice or whoever's, singing softly in a nasal tenor as clear as spring water, and then you recognized the song, one of John Denver's impossibly sentimental ballads about home and hearth and supper on the stove that you were always ashamed of liking, but you would not be taken that easily—street smart New Yorker—and you searched his bowed head for fraud, searched out his eyes even as you reached for your loose change, and just then the small pale man drew abreast of you and threw back his head, and as his eyes came up milky and twisted and wrong, his face fused ecstatically and the purest sound came forth from him and struck something inside you that came undone, and you would have given great value at that moment to see what he saw, to see what lay beyond embarrassment.

Razorburn

by Andrew J. Olson

Justene searched the bus for her best friend Abby. She saw Abby waving and so she quickly slid into the seat next to her as the bus jerked forward.

"You like my nails?" Abby asked, showcasing them to Justene. They were painted a dark shade of blue, but sparkled. They matched her blue, star-shaped earrings and blue socks.

Justene's mom wouldn't let her pierce her ears or paint her nails until next year, when she would be in sixth grade. Abby painted her nails a different color every week. Sometimes on the weekends Justene would help Abby paint her nails.

"Do you think Bobby will like them?" Abby asked.

Of course he will, Justene thought. All the boys had crushes on Abby, even the ones who came to school with manure on their boots and unwashed hair.

"I don't know," she said. "Maybe."

"Well, last Friday in the tires, Bobby told me that his favorite color was blue," Abby said.

Justene's face flushed as she looked out the frosted window. The tires were a bunch of old tractor tires stacked up behind the recreation building. Some of the girls in sixth grade said the boys sometimes went pee in the tires when they didn't want to go back inside during recess. Justene had also heard from Sarah that Abby had kissed Bobby in the tires. She thought about Bobby peeing in the tires and her cheeks warmed again.

"Abby…"

Abby looked at Justene and a small smile appeared on her face. Justene leaned in and cupped her hand over Abby's ear, her bottom lip brushing against the blue earring as she whispered, "Did you kiss Bobby in the tires?" Justene could feel Abby giggling they were sitting so close.

Abby quickly cupped her own hand over Justene's ear. "Yeah, me and Bobby are dating. Abby flicked one of her long bangs back, just like her mother.

Justene wished she could be more like Abby—more grown up, that's what the boys liked, and it seemed like so much fun, putting on nail polish and makeup, matching clothes to your earrings.

The bus pulled up to school and the girls walked to their homeroom, which was bustling. Mrs. Zimmer was sick and Principal Reed was going to substitute for the first half of the day.

"Please, please, everyone get situated and in your seats."

Abby looked at Justene and they both giggled. Some of the sixth-grade girls had said Principal Reed would give girls quarters to rub his shoulders. When he walked down the hallways, the coins would jingle in his pocket.

Abby flung off her boots and went off in stocking feet to show Bobby her nails. Justene couldn't slip her boot off and sat down. As she rolled up her jeans, Principal Reed walked over. Justene pulled the boot off.

"I like a girl with hairy legs," Principal Reed said as he gently touched Justene's shin.

Justene quickly covered her leg and quietly sat down in her seat. She looked at Abby who sat a few desks in front of her.

Justene knew that under those blue socks, Abby had smooth skin.

Rubbing her foot over her leg, Justene felt warm and ashamed. She stayed on the swings for recess and let Abby talk about Bobby the whole ride home. When she finally got to her house, Justene ran inside and locked herself in her parents' bathroom. She ran the bathtub and took out her mother's razor and cream. Justene began shaving her legs, small droplets of blood swirling in the bathwater.

Out of Kansas

by Nicole Borg

I have become that girl
speaking from behind the curtain—

It is Dorothy I think of and her yappy dog
befriending misfits, taking wrong turns,

trusting in fairy tales to get back home.
I've forgotten home, except in dreams—

the world tears up around me,
the farmhouse flies, and the dog won't stop yipping.

Someone died under a great weight,
someone was bitter and pissed-off and ached inside.

Sometimes, I think I'm the bitter one
or the crushed one or the girl who can't get back.

It's hard to tell with dreams.
Maybe I am none of these—

My heart has turned to tin. I've made an art of forgetting.
I'm always too quick to trust the loudest voice.

Less certain than a road of brick, I will walk a new path,
tracking that wild animal who is me.

I will feed her from my hand
and all that I've never said
               will come out in a roar.

Kindness

by Naomi Shihab Nye

Before you know what kindness really is
you must lose things,
feel the future dissolve in a moment
like salt in a weakened broth.
What you held in your hand,
what you counted and carefully saved,
all this must go so you know
how desolate the landscape can be
between the regions of kindness.
How you ride and ride
thinking the bus will never stop,
the passengers eating maize and chicken
will stare out the window forever.

Before you learn the tender gravity of kindness
you must travel where the Indian in a white poncho
lies dead by the side of the road.
You must see how this could be you,
how he too was someone
who journeyed through the night with plans
and the simple breath that kept him alive.

Before you know kindness as the deepest thing inside,
you must know sorrow as the other deepest thing.

You must wake up with sorrow.
You must speak to it till your voice
catches the thread of all sorrows
and you see the size of the cloth.

Then it is only kindness that makes sense anymore,
only kindness that ties your shoes
and sends you out into the day to gaze at bread,
only kindness that raises its head
from the crowd of the world to say
It is I you have been looking for,
and then goes with you everywhere
like a shadow or a friend.

The Refugees

by Linda LeGarde Grover

To the dirging of "The Way We Were"
sung by some sweet girl nobody knows
six pallbearers
two in sweatshirts with washed away logos
three in second-hand dress shirts
one in a borrowed sportcoat
carry above their bowlegged lockstep mince
the flocked vinyl coffin out the side door. Inside
our beloved mother, grandma and aunt rests,
megis shell on a black string
wound over her bent brown fingers.

Six pallbearers worn as their boot heels
and ground to unassuming humility
by the rounds of looking for work
and sometimes finding it bravely
wear their bodies as a single suit of clothes
fraying fast and worn at the knees.
These are the faces of outside work, aging young skin
tanned by the sun and creased
ever more deeply season to season
filled and emptied filled and emptied
with grime and hard living that
search then escape what they've found

spending night after numb night on a stool at Mr. J's
thinking, maybe after one more
I'll ask that blonde or her friend to dance;
no, guess I'll just go home, after all.

This is what really happened to the other Indians,
not the noble savage beauties you watch
on made-for-TV movies, running in crisp, freshly ironed
loincloths through a pristine forest full of friendly animals
with an important message for the Chief
from his daughter the Princess,
who enthrall you so with their simple ways
(*"oh wow these people are just so close to nature,
to SPEAR-itual—I wannabe, I wanna have"*)
that you can buy at a craft show stand
along with some gen-yew-whine turquoise and silver
jewelry so that you can be an Indian, too.

No, we're the other Indians,
the ones who did our time in boarding school
where we learned to take a beating
never quite mastered forced English
learned the work ethic and what it meant for us
but survived, more or less, in spite of it.

We moved to town, refugees we became
displaced persons scorned by our own people.
Our daughters married white men

and learned to take a beating
never quite mastered Anglo housekeeping
lived the work ethic and for them it meant
they would grow old early *our daughters*
beloved and revered the bearers of life
and generations to come how could we protect them,
our daughters whose spirits tired and whose
blue-eyed children went to public school
and learned to take a beating
as well as give one in return
never mastered school work,
leaving when they turned sixteen,
having learned what the work ethic meant for them
so they too could live hard and grow old early.

And today we're at another funeral,
and since it's the mortuary's rock bottom budget
package deal we move outside the Sunset Chapel
once our hour is up. We're grateful
for this warm and sunny day
and for room on the sidewalk
for cousins to meet and talk
("ain't seen you since the last funeral")
til the chapel needs the sidewalk back
and we head for Mr. J's.

Our beloved is gone she has traveled
her four day spirit walk

and has arrived west.
Her corpse waits in a flocked vinyl coffin
on a shelf in the mortuary's garage
for the off-hours ride to the cemetery,
megis shell on a black string
wound over her bent brown fingers.

I Was Never Able To Pray

by Edward Hirsch

Wheel me down to the shore
where the lighthouse was abandoned
and the moon tolls in the rafters.

Let me hear the wind paging through the trees
and see the stars flaring out, one by one,
like the forgotten faces of the dead.

I was never able to pray,
but let me inscribe my name
in the book of waves

and then stare into the dome
of a sky that never ends
and see my voice sail into the night.

Afterword: Salad on the Theme of Succotash

by Deborah Jacobs

Start with summer: a garden, a sky-high sun, gentle rain, and the miracle of lima beans and corn and a fat red onion all ready on the same good day.

Blanch the corn, not too long. With your sharpest, gentlest knife slice down the cobs; watch the plump rows of fat, milky, kernels slide off and pile up. Try not to weep at their generosity. Not yet. Steam or carefully simmer the limas to their plump, just-before-bursting softness. Resist the desire to melt them in your mouth one after another. Let the beans cool. Meanwhile, slice thin as paper the fragrant red onion. Enjoy the spray your sharp knife releases. Weep now. Wash the sturdy field greens (baby anything just won't do). Spin or shake them dry. Whisk together your best salad oil, champagne vinegar, the juice of an orange, s & p.

With a light hand (no bruising allowed), toss everything together in a large bowl. Let every contributor shine even while this mixing results in a new iteration. [This is excellent advice for anthologists as well. And for community builders. And for democracies.]

Use real dishes. Eat outdoors.

Contributors

Marvin Bell's twenty-four books include *Vertigo: The Living Dead Man Poems, Mars Being Red, Nightworks: Poems 1962-2000,* and *After the Fact: Scripts & Postscripts*, a dialogue with Christopher Merrill. Forthcoming in 2019 is *Incarnate: The Collected Dead Man Poems*. He lives in Iowa City, Iowa, and also for 34 years in Port Townsend, Washington. He is known for his many collaborations with other artists, and his writing has been called "ambitious without pretension."

Wendell Berry is a renowned poet, novelist, essayist, environmentalist, and cultural and economic critic. He lives in Port Royal, Kentucky near his birthplace, where he has maintained a farm for over 40 years. He is the author of over 40 books of poetry, fiction, and essays.

Nicole Borg is an English teacher, editor, and poet, who is enamored with place: the plains of ND, the Rocky Mountains, the desert of CA, and the high desert of CO. Her first collection of poetry *All Roads Lead Home* published in 2018 by Up on Big Rock Poetry Series, an imprint of *Shipwreckt Books*, is like a poetry road trip. Nicole lives along the lovely Mississippi River in Minnesota with her husband and two sons.

Aaron Brown is the author of the poetry collection, *Acacia Road*, winner of the 2016 Gerald Cable Book Award (Silverfish Review Press). He has been published in *World Literature Today, Tupelo*

Quarterly, Waxwing, Cimarron Review, and *Transition*, among others, and he is a contributing editor for *Windhover* and blogs regularly for *Ruminate*. Brown grew up in Chad and now lives in Kansas, where he is a professor of writing at Sterling College. He holds an MFA from the University of Maryland.

Jane Brox's most recent book is *Silence: A Social History of One of the Least Understood Elements of Our Lives*, which has been named an Editors' Choice by The New York Times. She has written four others, including *Brilliant: The Evolution of Artificial Light* and *Five Thousand Days Like This One*, which was a finalist for the National Book Critics Circle Award. She lives in Maine.

Kathy Fish teaches for the Mile High MFA at Regis University in Denver CO. She has published five collections of short fiction, most recently *Wild Life: Collected Works from 2003-2018* (Matter Press). More information at kathy-fish.com.

Julie Gard's prose poetry collections include *Home Studies* (New Rivers Press), a finalist for the 2016 Minnesota Book Award, *Scrap: On Louise Nevelson* (Ravenna Press), and two chapbooks. Her poems, stories, and essays have appeared in *Gertrude, Fourth River, Clackamas Literary Review, Crab Orchard Review, Ekphrasis and Blackbox Manifold*, among other journals and anthologies. She lives in Duluth, Minnesota and is Associate Professor of Writing at the University of Wisconsin-Superior. www.juliegard.com

Ross Gay is the author, most recently, of *Catalog of Unabashed Gratitude* and *The Book of Delights*. He works on The Tenderness Project with Shayla Lawson (tendernesses.com) and teaches at Indiana University.

Nancy Miller Gomez's work has appeared or is forthcoming in *River Styx, Rattle, The Massachusetts Review, The Bellingham Review, Verse Daily, American Life in Poetry*, and elsewhere. She was a semi-finalist for the Pablo Neruda Poetry Prize. Her chapbook, "*Punishment*" was published as part of the *Rattle* Chapbook Series. She has an MFA from Pacific University and volunteers with The Santa Cruz Poetry Project, an organization that provides poetry workshops to incarcerated men and women.

Linda LeGarde Grover is a professor of American Indian studies at the University of Minnesota Duluth and a member of the Bois Forte Band of Ojibwe. Her novel *The Road Back to Sweetgrass* received the Wordcraft Circle of Native Writers and Storytellers Fiction Award, her essay collection *Onigamiising: Seasons of an Ojibwe Year* the 2018 Minnesota Book Award for Memoir and Creative Nonfiction and the Northeastern Minnesota Book Award.

Edward Hirsch's tenth book of poems, *Stranger By Night*, will be published by Knopf in 2020. He has also published five prose books, among them, *How to Read a Poem and Fall in Love with Poetry*, a national bestseller. He lives in Brooklyn.

Debra Marquart is the author of six books including *Small Buried Things: Poems* and *The Horizontal World: Growing Up Wild in the Middle of Nowhere*. Marquart is a recipient of an NEA Fellowship, a PEN USA Award, and Elle Magazine's Elle Lettres Award. She teaches in the MFA Program in Creative Writing and Environment at Iowa State University and the Stonecoast Low-Residency Program at the University of Southern Maine.

Siri Liv Myhrom is a freelance writer and editor living in Minneapolis, MN. When not writing, she likes to explore her state's remaining wild spaces, in all seasons, with her husband and two young daughters. She is currently finishing a collection of essays and prose poems on grief called *Even If They're A Crowd of Sorrows*. The essayette, "Peonies," is part of that work.

Naomi Shihab Nye has written or edited more than 30 books and has been a visiting writer for many years in schools and communities all over the world. A graduate of Trinity University, she lives in San Antonio.

Andrew J. Olson grew up in a small town in west central Minnesota and holds an MFA from Minnesota State University Moorhead. He is an English professor at Northeastern Oklahoma A&M College where he lives with his wife and daughter. Andrew's work has appeared in numerous journals across the U.S. from Seattle to Brooklyn.

Octavio Solis is a playwright whose newest play, *Mother Road*, recently premiered at the Oregon Shakespeare Festival. His fiction has been published in the *Chicago Quarterly Review, Catamaran Literary Reader, Eleven Eleven*, the *Louisville Review, Huizache, Arroyo Literary Review* and *Zyzzyva*. *Retablos* is his first book.

Don Shea's stories have appeared in many venues including *The Gettysburg Review, The North American Review, The Quarterly*, and 3 Norton Anthologies. He has been twice nominated for a Pushcart Prize and has long experience teaching writing workshops at the YMCA and Bard High School Early College.

Thomas Stetzler is an itinerant harmonicist and poet who wandered from institution to institution, job to job on the trail out of youth until he discovered the right therapist, who led him into recovery. Then his poems began to appear in regional publications. A forthcoming chapbook, *Seeing in the Dark*, will be released in the summer of 2019. Presently, he lives in solitude in Park Rapids, Minnesota.

Rosemerry Wahtola Trommer served as the third Colorado Western Slope Poet Laureate (2015-2017), co-hosts Emerging Form (a podcast on creative process) and co-directs Telluride's Talking Gourds Poetry Club. Her poetry has appeared in *O Magazine*, on *A Prairie Home Companion*, in *Rattle.com*, and on river rocks. Her most recent collection is *Naked for Tea* (Able Muse Press, 2018). She teaches poetry for 12-step recovery programs, hospice, mindfulness retreats, and women's retreats. Mantra: adjust www.wordwoman.com

John Edgar Wideman is the author of more than twenty works of fiction and nonfiction, including the award-winning *Brothers and Keepers*, *Philadelphia Fire*, and *Writing to Save a Life*. His honors include a MacArthur Fellowship, two PEN/ Faulkner Awards, and an O. Henry Award and nominations for the National Book Award and the National Book Critics Circle Award.

Permissions

"The Revolution Needs a Song" by Marvin Bell, from *After the Fact: Scripts & Postscripts*, by Marvin Bell and Christopher Merrill. White Pine Press, 2016. Reprinted by permission of the publisher.

"The Peace of Wild Things" by Wendell Berry. Copyright © 2012 by Wendell Berry, from *New Collected Poems*. Reprinted by permission of Counterpoint Press.

"Out of Kansas" by Nicole Borg. Copyright © 2018 by Nicole Borg. Previously published in her collection *All Roads Lead Home* (Up On Big Rock Poetry Series, a Shipwreckt Books imprint, 2018). Reprinted by permission of the author.

"Elegy" by Aaron Brown. Copyright © 2018 by Aaron Brown. From *Acacia Road* (Silverfish Review Press, 2018). Reprinted by permission of the author.

"Star Light, Star Bright" by Jane Brox, first published in OnEarth (the magazine of The National Resources Defense Council), online and in print. Reprinted by permission of the author.

"Collective Nouns for Humans in the Wild" by Kathy Fish. Copyright © 2017 by Kathy Fish. From *Jellyfish Review* (October 13, 2017). Reprinted in *The Best Small Fictions* 2018, edited by Aimee Bender and Sherrie Flick (Braddock Avenue Books, 2018) and *Best American Nonrequired Reading* 2018, edited by Sheila Heti (NY: HMH, 2018). Used with permission of the author.

"On Scarcity" and "Homage to Lydia Davis" by Julie Gard. From *Home Studies* (New Rivers Press, 2015). Reprinted by permission. "On Scarcity" also appeared in *When We Become Weavers: Queer Female Poets on the Midwestern Experience* (Squares and Rebels Press, 2012).

"What About That, Steve Jobs?" by Ross Gay. Copyright © 2019 by Ross Gay. Published here for the first time.

"Growing Apples" by Nancy Miller Gomez, from *Punishment* by Nancy Miller Gomez. Rattle Foundation, 2018. Reprinted by permission of the author.

"The Refugees" by Linda LeGarde Grover. Copyright © 2001 by Linda LeGarde Grover. From *The Sky Watched: Poems of Ojibwe Lives* (Red Mountain Press 2015). Reprinted by permission of the author.

"I Was Never Able to Pray" by Edward Hirsch. Copyright © 2010 by Edward Hirsch. From *The Northwest Review*, Vol.48, No.2. Reprinted by permission of the author.

"Dylan's Lost Years" by Debra Marquart from *The Hunger Bone: Rock and Roll Stories* (New Rivers Press, 2001). Reprinted in *NEW MICRO: Exceptionally Short Fiction*, edited by James

Thomas and Robert Scotellar (W.W. Norton, 2018). Reprinted by permission of the author.

"Peonies" by Siri Liv Myhrom. Copyright © 2019 by Siri Liv Myhrom. Published here for the first time.

"Kindness" by Naomi Shihab Nye, from *Words Under the Words: Selected Poems* by Naomi Shihab Nye, copyright © 1995. Reprinted with permission of Far Corner Books.

"Razorburn" by Andrew J. Olson. Copyright © 2013 by Andrew J. Olson. First published in *Barn Stripping and Other Stories* (Outskirts Press 2013). Reprinted by permission of the author.

"Blindsided" by Don Shea from Crescent Review 13:2. Reprinted in *NEW MICRO: Exceptionally Short Fiction*, edited by James Thomas and Robert Scotellar (W.W. Norton, 2018). Used by permission of the author.

"*La Migra*" by Octavio Solis, from *Retablos: Stories From a Life Lived Along the Border*. Copyright © 2018 by Octavio Solis. Reprinted with the permission of The Permissions Company LLC on behalf of City Lights Books, www.citylights.com.

"Meditation" and "Spectator" by Thomas C. Stetzler. Copyright © 2009 by Thomas C. Stetzler. From *Waiting for the Darkness to Lose Interest* (North Star Press, 2009). Reprinted by permission of the author.

"Perhaps You Can Hear It?" by Rosemerry Wahtola Trommer. Copyright © 2018 by Rosemerry Wahtola Trommer. Previously published in *A Hundred Falling Veils*. Reprinted by permission of the author.

"Witness," currently collected in *BRIEFS*, by John Edgar Wideman. Copyright © 2010 by John Edgar Wideman, used by permission of The Wylie Agency LLC.

About the Editor

Deborah Jacobs has been a literature professor, a restaurateur, a long-term caregiver, an arts administrator, and a professional singer; she is also a lifelong road tripper, baseball fan, gardener, and indie bookstore junkie. In October 2018, she founded Danielle Dufy Literary and its imprint French Press Editions. She lives in central Minnesota with her husband, Bill, on one of the most beautiful lakes in the world.

Acknowledgements

First thanks go to Michele, my assistant in all things (editorial and otherwise). Thank you for stepping out of your retirement to help me chase this dream. Every dreamer should be so lucky to have a sister like you who has her back. Your detail-oriented, meticulous nature makes me a better editor; your generosity makes me a better person. Thank you.

To Judith, for believing in my vision; for listening patiently (usually between customers at Scout & Morgan), even to ideas that were barely formed; for stepping up your support as that vision gained clarity; for asking the right questions and for occasionally offering judicious advice; for generously paving my way with other booksellers; and for your continued enthusiastic cheerleading on my behalf. I am deeply grateful.

To Chip and Jean at River Place Press, thank you dear friends for instantly recognizing *Stone Gathering* as a worthy and necessary project; for generously offering your skills, wisdom, and resources to help bring it to fruition; for honoring my determination to be a publisher and to start my own small press, for graciously agreeing to mentor me, to provide the design and layout for *Stone Gathering*, and to shepherd it through printing—all this without any proprietary interest, without any need to tout your own press's logo or credentials. Not many established professionals would step back in this way, even as they offer everything they have to someone else's project. But you did. And by doing so, you let my own brand come to the fore, my own small press announce itself to the world, my own reputation shine. I love you for this and for a multitude of things that won't show up in this paragraph. Thank you.

To Nick and Andy, my boys (boys? now both in your late 30s). How is it you are somehow always as proud of your mother as she is of you? You shore me up, over and over again. Thank you.

And to Bill, my man of few words (which is okay, since I have so many). You are the grand prize of my life; you are my launching pad, my compass, my homing device, and my refuge. Thank you for your unwavering support for everything I do, for everything I am, and for everything I am becoming. I love you.

About French Press Editions

French Press Editions is an imprint of Danielle Dufy Literary, a company dedicated to celebrating literary short forms, widening their readership, and supporting independent bookstores for whom they can be a hard sell.

French Press Editions are small-format (5x7), 72-page, perfect-bound paperback books, priced at $10.95. They are marketed as *portable, affordable, collectible literature* and are available exclusively through independent booksellers and by subscription.

In addition to *Stone Gathering: A Reader* (a quarterly collection of short-form literature), French Press Editions publishes an annual stand-alone short-form collection on a special theme. *The Relevance of the Rural: A Tribute to Wendell Berry* is planned for late January 2020.

faces, the edge in the eyes, it's all the same, only now the faces and eyes are brown. The badges say Marquez, Armendariz, Lujan. Some are even rougher than their Anglo counterparts. It doesn't matter that their parents probably came over the same river with the same intention; one generation is all it takes to keep the past and the legacy of their migration at bay. They're American now and this is how they show it.

We're used to them, how they slow down whenever we're outside drinking Cokes by our bikes. The officer in his Aviator sunglasses looks us over, scouring our skinny bodies for the one thing that marks us as foreign. Kino and I point to each other and mouth the words: take him, take him. My sister takes exception, though. She thinks the border cop is checking her out, and she's probably right. But the fact that he's even scrutinizing us this closely is disturbing. His look lingers just long enough to make us feel like strangers to ourselves. All the *mojaditos* that we generally scowl at when we spy them tramping restlessly past our house; he's consciously connecting them to us. We're nothing like them, we've conditioned ourselves to say. We're legal, born on this side. But the border cop with his steady gaze is telling us with his look that the distinction is very thin. Thin as the lenses on his Aviators. Thin as a line on a map.

This day I am waiting for the bus to take me downtown to see a movie. The bus stop is just across the street from my house. The Border Patrol comes up the street and stops right at the curb. It's that Mexican officer again and he's wearing the same reflective shades. His partner is this white guy who looks like he's been badly sunburned. Both of them are giving me a once-over that makes me nervous. It's the Mexican who talks to me.

You seen anyone go by here lately?

No.

Anyone wearing a red tee?

No.

You're wearing a red tee.

I look down at myself and look at the red tee-shirt with the lettering of some band I used to think was bitchen.

Where you from, kid, he asks.

Here.

Where.

America.

Where do you live?

Right there. I point at my house.

What's the address?

I recite it for him like my life depends on it.

Then he does something unexpected. He removes his shades and asks me, *¿Hablas español?*

Now I'm trapped. I want to say no, even if it's a lie. 'Cause to admit that I speak Spanish would put me in the other guy's red tee. Just like that, he's made me ashamed of my original tongue, forced me to deny my father's language and thereby deny my father and his fathers before him. And the crazy thing about it is this man is using that very same Spanish against me. There's only one thing I can say.

A little.

¿Quieres pasar tus días allí?

What?

You know what I said.

No sir.

He smirks at my lie and looks me right in the face. Do you want to spend your days over there?

I'm an American, sir.

Barely. Where you going?

The movies.

In my peripheral vision, I sense my mom at the front door and the white officer nudges his partner, who puts on his Aviators and tells me to keep an eye out for a *mojado* with a red tee-shirt. Which is what I see reflected in the lenses.

If you spot him, you call us, okay?

These guys are the butts of our jokes. Now they have me shaking all over. They say, Have a good day and drive on down the street. The bus comes right after they leave and I go to my James Bond double bill at the Palace Theatre downtown, and the whole time I'm watching the screen, I am hating these men and thanking them at the same time. Because they're right. I am the guy in the red tee. I am him. And he is me.

Elegy

by Aaron Brown

We were supposed
to become old men:

our wives mingling
as friends,

grinding millet
to powder over

the conversation
of stifling afternoons,

and our children
giggling meanwhile,

shooting marbles
and flipping cards—

the games we used to
play not too long ago.

We were supposed
to be two old men,

sharing
in the silence

of empty tea glasses,
laughing at God's humor

instead of just me
wondering

why he'd want you
when I still do.

Witness

by John Edgar Wideman

Sitting here one night six floors up on my little balcony when I heard shots and saw them boys running. My eyes went straight to the lot beside Mason's bar and I saw something black not moving in the weeds and knew a body lying there and knew it was dead. A fifteen-year-old boy the papers said. Whole bunch of sirens and cops and spinning lights the night I'm talking about. I watched till after they rolled him away and then everything got quiet again as it ever gets round here so I'm sure the boy's people not out there that night. Didn't see them till next morning when I'm looking down at those weeds and a couple's coming slow on Frankstown with a girl by the hand, had to be the boy's baby sister. They pass terrible Mason's and stop right at the spot the boy died. Then they commence to swaying, bowing, hugging, waving their arms about. Forgive me, Jesus, but look like they grief dancing, like the sidewalk too cold or too hot they had to jump around not to burn up. How'd his people find the exact spot. Did they hear my old mind working to lead them, guide them along like I would if I could get up out this damn wheelchair and take them by the hand.

Homage to Lydia Davis

by Julie Gard

A was done with B's rudeness, and because B would not write an apology note to A, C refused to help blow-dry B's hair. The problem this time was B's shirt, which A felt was too low-cut when B leaned over. As C in this situation I agreed, yet based on observation of area teens, found the neckline within current standards of decency. Of course, as one of two mothers bracketing B, I would have preferred that the neckline be higher. As C, I would certainly not have allowed it to go any lower. And so A was tired of the rudeness, the meanness, and C was ashamed that it still went on, while B was simply unhappy with wet hair, eating granola bars for breakfast and reading the funnies. In other news, a power plant in Connecticut exploded while workers were clearing the gas lines and the whole thing plumed like a hibachi grill. Five men died—let's call them D through H—replacing A, B and C altogether in this story.

On Scarcity

by Julie Gard

We are short a pair of brown shoes in our house. My partner put them on this morning and I'd already dressed in brown pants, striped socks and a nice green shirt; all I needed were the shoes she was already wearing. I can't believe she took them off. I can't believe I asked her to. It's true they're mine, but I would cut out a kidney for her, even a lung, and so why not give her the shoes? They are perfectly wide and comfortable. She is older, smarter, and doesn't have as many nightmares. We should have better boundaries, at least different-sized feet. We should plan better. She says that it happens on Thursdays. There is something about the end of the week, when everything starts running out.

Dylan's Lost Years

by Debra Marquart

Somewhere between Hibbing and New York, the red rust streets of the Iron Range and the shipping yards of the Atlantic, somewhere between Zimmerman and Dylan was a pit stop in Fargo, a Superman-in-the-phone-booth interlude, recalled by no one but the Danforth brothers, who hired the young musician, fresh in town with his beat-up six-string and his small-town twang, to play shake, rattle, and roll, to play good golly, along with Wayne on the keys and Dirk on the bass, two musical brothers whom you might still find playing the baby grand, happy hours at the southside Holiday Inn.

And if you slip the snifter a five, Wayne might talk between how high the moon, and embraceable you, about Dylan's lost years, about the Elvis sneer, the James Dean leather collar pulled tight around his neck, about the late-night motorcycle rides, kicking over the city's garbage cans, and how they finally had to let him go, seeing how he was more trouble than he was worth, and with everyone in full agreement that the new boy just could not sing.

What About That, Steve Jobs?

by Ross Gay

This morning, about 7:30, I was drinking coffee at a window seat of the restaurant in the hotel where I'm staying in New York. (Oh, I should say, yesterday I mentioned as a postscript to an introduction to a poem of mine that involves planting my father's ashes with some plum trees, during which I always ask if anyone has done anything with their placenta, as a lure for someone to say "I planted a tree with mine!" which happens often, though not here, and the postscript to the prescript was that my partner Stephanie had every intention of doing something with hers, though busy I guess tossed it in the freezer for later deciding. That placenta [and child] are now nineteen years old, and hiding somewhere, I suspect, in the freezer [placenta, not child], though I don't know a lot about placentas, couldn't necessarily spot one from far away, or close up for that matter, nor could I necessarily tell if it looked much like the bananas that had been in there for a while, a bit freezer-burnt, which, you know, and I needed bananas for a smoothie. There was much gasping and "nooooooooo!"ing, and much relief when I revealed the bananas were in fact bananas. I think.)

A woman sat down a couple tables away, wearing all the best colors—a kind of peach tunic, a woven magenta shawl, green scarf. She looked maybe a bit old to be the mother of the child who joined her, I thought, then quickly thought that is a simple and simplistic notion of parenthood and age and probably even biology. Simplistic many things. What do I know? Pardon me. When he sat down a true soul tune was thumping the radio, and he bounced and drummed on the sides of his chair, and his mother joined him, her head bobbing like a buoy. They were speaking a language that I think has some intermittent English, and how lovely it felt to be in an actual and psychic space in America where I don't expect English. The mother has given the boy periodic instructions, not necessarily oppressive (this is my issue, I know, I know), just little this and that—one such instruction had to do with how to order his tea, something about milk tea I think, be sure this and that, though I couldn't quite tell. Their closeness—dancing, smirking, teaching, learning—has been replaced with their interactions, both of them, with their cellular telephones. Can I say it plainly? Fuck Steve Jobs. I hear he was a genuine dick, but I'm talking about the intimacy-wonder-quiet-conversation-murderer his gizmo is. I know he doesn't deserve all the credit, and he's dead, but fuck him still.

When we were kids, and our dad was toting us somewhere in the Brown Car (78 Toyota Corolla Hatchback, a chariot of transcendent beauty, *The Chariot of Transcendent Beauty*) one of us must've reached for the wiper fluid button, for it was a button, and any button, to a child, is for pushing until it breaks, especially a button with the very pretty image someone invented of a spray of liquid that looked on the seductive little button like a fountain—I think I understood the word skatepark from my phone-studying neighbors—an image my father, always on his toes, promptly told us was in fact a flower, which to a four and six year old the image, yup, could be a flower. Especially to some kids to whom anything spoken by our father was true. And if we were to push the button, he told us, the car would turn into a flower.

Which sounds badass, and truly an intervention into the carbon morass we've made. If cars could be turned into flowers, probably airplanes could be turned into trees. And factories into forests. And on and on. Lest you think I'm hagiographizing my dad, I will tell you, too, that the flower in his formulation was a warning, because it would draw a giant bee that would sting us. I am happy to say I am a beekeeper, and am generally bee and bugphilic, so that potential damage was averted. But I am even happier to tell you that for years—years and years—I knew that by pushing a button a car could be turned into a flower. What about that, Steve Jobs, you fucking genius?

The Revolution Needs a Song

by Marvin Bell

When events occur for which there are only insufficient words, when movement is forbidden, when there is only an odor of ash in darkness, when every sense has been stifled, when we wake in chains, there remains a simmering of song, a residue in which a microscopic ferment has already begun. Take two chopsticks on a countertop, a comb between two scraps of paper, two spoons to slap against a knee, a length of vinyl hose into which one has wedged a mouthpiece. If it causes you to sing or dance, if it pumps your heart or fills your lungs or rattles your spine, then you are, for the nonce, in the realm of the infinite no-mind, carried by a progression of changes. Now anything can happen. Never mind the key sign, the metronome, the trumpet players counting rests while the strings fill the hall. Never mind the danger to the long-time oboist, the bruised lips of the brass players, the stiffening fingers of the pianists. Forget that the players make music at a high personal cost. That's the profession. I am speaking here of the nature of rhythm, pitch, melody, phrasing and harmony. The five food groups of the soul. Take a tingly triangle, a horsey woodblock, bowls full of tympani, the simplicity of a pipe with valves, the sonorous metalwork of a steel drum, a fretless washtub bass. The barest rhythm or tune can imprison or free us, and the words of songs, like dreams, are incontestable. Music always wins.

Growing Apples

by Nancy Miller Gomez

There is big excitement in C block today.
On the window sill,
in a plastic ice cream cup
a little plant is growing.
This is all the men want to talk about:
how an apple seed germinated
in a crack of damp concrete;
how they tore open tea bags
to collect the leaves, leached them
in water, then laid the sprout onto the bed
made of Lipton. How this finger of spring
dug one delicate root down
into the dark fannings and now
two small sleeves of green
are pushing out from the emerging tip.
The men are tipsy with this miracle.
Each morning, one by one,
they go to the window and check
the progress of the struggling plant.
All through the day they return
to stand over the seedling
and whisper.

Collective Nouns for Humans in the Wild

by Kathy Fish

A group of grandmothers is a *tapestry*. A group of toddlers, a *jubilance* (see also: a *bewailing*). A group of librarians is an *enlightenment*. A group of visual artists is a *bioluminescence*. A group of short story writers is a *Flannery*. A group of musicians is—a *band*.

A *resplendence* of poets.
A *beacon* of scientists.
A *raft* of social workers.

A group of first responders is a *valiance*. A group of peaceful protestors is a *dream*. A group of special education teachers is a *transcendence*. A group of neonatal ICU nurses is a *divinity*. A group of hospice workers, a *grace*.

Humans in the wild, gathered and feeling good, previously an *exhilaration*, now: a *target*.

A *target* of concert-goers.
A *target* of movie-goers.
A *target* of dancers.

A group of schoolchildren is a *target*.

The Peace of Wild Things

by Wendell Berry

When despair grows in me
and I wake in the night at the least sound
in fear of what my life and my children's lives may be,
I go and lie down where the wood drake
rests in his beauty on the water, and the great heron feeds.
I come into the peace of wild things
who do not tax their lives with forethought
of grief. I come into the presence of still water.
And I feel above me the day-blind stars
waiting for their light. For a time
I rest in the grace of the world, and am free.

Star Light, Star Bright

by Jane Brox

I am beginning to forget things about the island where I once lived, and the remote house on a dirt road where I spent two winters more than twenty-five years ago. I'm not sure anymore how long the ferry ride from the mainland was, or when the scallop season started. I've lost the names of acquaintances. But the one thing I'll never forget is the night sky above my home those winter nights, which I anticipated as I drove out of town with its bright clusters of shop windows and then outdistanced the last of the streetlights.

Beyond their glare the road narrowed and the human lights grew more and more sparse until, when I turned down my rutted road, my own headlights were all I had to orient me in the dark. Once I arrived home and turned them off, I often couldn't see my hand in front of my face, certainly not when the moon was down. I always was aware of the phases of the moon then. There would be more stars than dark, just as Chekhov once wrote—so many stars one could not have put a finger in between them—and they seemed close enough to reach up and touch. Even so, I didn't have to look skyward to feel their presence. I sensed their weight—that's the only way I can describe it—a kind of pressure bearing down on me.

As much as I tried, I found it almost impossible to stand and ponder them for long, for as beautiful as they were, they also made me apprehensive. Part of that may have been my own young solitary self in that remote corner. It may have been the cold and the wind. All I know is that I encountered those stars each time with mixed feelings of awe and loneliness, and often I hastened to feel for my keys and then the lock on the door. Once I moved inside, I saw to everything that would cut me off from the outer night—the lights, the fire, the radio, supper—the small tasks that people turn to so as to make themselves at home.

Still, the feeling I had beneath the stars lingered long into the evening. How must it have been for so much of human time when people had almost no way to take cover from the night—no more than a smoky fire or a lone candle that at its best also smoked, and stank, and lit only a meal, a face, a hand? Not much to do after a while but talk on in the dark, and then sleep.

Now I live in the heart of a modest town, so, like most people in this country, I don't see many stars anymore, and the sky between them isn't really dark. The streetlights outside my windows are so bright I can wander through my house without turning on a lamp. I see illuminated windows in every direction; the neighborhood forms its own constellation of far, near, bright, dim, upstairs, downstairs, which carries its own kind of beauty. When I walk through the streets at night I notice the moon above the windows and street lamps, and can sometimes spy a planet or a major constellation—Orion, Cassiopeia—more easily than I ever could before. The sparse stars feel familiar, part of the neighborhood, although they seem much farther away than they did on the island, and I never feel the pressure of them.

Sometimes I try to imagine the night sky I once knew shining above the town, as if starlight and human light could coexist with

La Migra

by Octavio Solis

THAT'S WHAT WE CALL THEM. That's how I have always known them. *La migra* is a derogatory term, but we don't even think of it like that. It's just what they are. Ever since we moved into the Lower Valley, the green and white cruisers of the Border Patrol have been everyday fixtures in our lives.

In the early days, they are older guys who take their jobs in stride. They ride on patrol like hired cowboys roping in the errant dogies. Or maybe more like Texas Rangers patrolling the wild frontier. They know a large portion of the migrants will slip through their net, and they know many of those they catch will be back through the fence in a matter of days. They're philosophical about their mission. What's the harm in a few *mojados* coming through? Don't we need the manpower anyway?

Then in the late '60s and early '70s, there's a new breed of officer. Stern all-American types, ex-soldiers who got their asses kicked in the jungles of Vietnam and now look to settle that score with these wetbacks and their smuggled maryjane. They take the job seriously, consider themselves a cut above the average city cop. What they do is harder and makes a bigger difference in the complicated world of *la frontera*. That's my take on them, anyway.

I start noticing something else in the early '70s, though. Maybe it was always there and I just didn't see it, or maybe it's a result of the recession and the lack of good-paying jobs. Suddenly there are more *Chicanos* manning the vans and cruisers. The iron in the

Perhaps You Can Hear It?

by Rosemerry Wahtola Trommer

Whatever an open field has always tried to say,
that's what I long to say to you. That, and the blue thrill
that trills in the larkspur just before it blooms.

And the communion of threads in the blanket,
the sincerity of wild strawberries, and
whatever it is that lavender says to the nose—

those are the notes I would write into the song
I'm still learning to sing, this song I would tuck
into your back pocket so that you might,

in the middle of a day, perhaps, find it there,
like stars behind the blue noon sky
just waiting for their time to emerge.